AF570742

FAREWELL TO THE BODY

FAREWELL TO THE BODY

Barbara Moore

The Word Works
Washington, DC

First Edition
First Printing
Farewell to the Body

Printed in the U.S.A.
Typography by Kathryn E. King/Dual Design
Cover photograph, *Lamentation*, by Carole Clem
Book design by Ronna Hammer

Library of Congress Number: 90-071210
International Standard Book Number: 0-915380-27-7

A number of poems in this book have appeared in the following journals: *The American Poetry Review*, Seeing; *Antioch Review*, Van Gogh; *The Bennington Review*, Crows Are Impossible in Heaven; *Cutbank*, Child Setting the Table for Breakfast, Braque Said; *The Georgia Review*, Almost Greek; *Hollins Critic*, Hanging Loose; *Kansas Quarterly*, Homing; *The Literary Review*, In Gratitude to Pissaro for His Woman and Child at the Well; *Massachusetts Review*, Carnival, City; *Midwest Quarterly*, River, Suburbs; *Minnesota Review*, Imagining Freedom; *Missouri Review*, Angel; *North American Review*, Room by Moonlight; *New Orleans Review*, Driving Home in Winter; *North Dakota Quarterly*, November; *Poetry*, Photograph Album, To the Orphans; *Salmagundi*, Crowed Up; *Slant*, What I Have to Say about Death; *Southwest Review*, These Days; *Southern Humanities Review*, For Luke Moore; *Tar River Poetry*, Evening Enjambed with Sparrows, In a Corner of Toulouse Lautrec; *Williwaw*, Coming out of the Movies, Such Afternoons, The Inn, The Rose Arriving. October received a prize from the BBC in 1981.

Farewell to the Body is the winner of the 1990 Word Works Washington Prize. Barbara Moore's manuscript was selected from more than 560 manuscripts submitted by American poets.

FIRST READERS:

Jamie Brown
Geraldine Connolly
Michael Davis
Howard Gofreed
Pat Gray
Lorraine Hollen De Perez
Jean Johnson
Elizabeth Jones
Peggy Miller
Gail Ranadive
Jodi Suleiman
Ian Walton
Jennifer Weinblatt
Leslie Wilson
Hastings Wyman

SECOND READERS:

Laura Fargas
Catherine Harnett Shaw
Sue Teigen

FINAL JUDGES:

Karren Alenier
J. H. Beall
Barbara Goldberg
Robert Sargent
Ronald Wilson, Project Director

Contents

III

IV

RIVER

In the blue mud of the river
where everything collects, we go
looking for our lives.
They are there, grave and radiant,
rising from the redundant clutter,
the bedsprings, the aching, rusty bolts.
Washed down in the mud of sleep
we turn on our losses,
the green stick of youth
still whittling itself under water,
the faces we love, rounding
into white stones.
We wake in our skins, still
feeling the smack of the river,
its tremor and traction.
Those rinsings and cullings
which accompany us through every night.

I

The Inn

The rain doesn't let up, or the snow,
it's always weather. Which is
why we stop exhausted at nightfall
and knock on the door of a dubious place.
Any place,
a place like an inn in Chekhov,
with dirty floors, dirtier icons,
finding a curious company there.
Wind howls in the stove, we draw together,
a curious company—a peasant,
a doctor, a vendor, whatever,
our faces equally hardened by our lives.
And gradually begin to tell our stories,
warmed by the vodka and salted cucumber,
our ghosts collecting with ruddy faces.

Strange how at home we feel.
Though our hearts are not good, and
we're horse stealers, every one of us,
we find ourselves suddenly happy,
going to sleep on the benches
lining the walls. Never minding
how hard they are, how lumpy the coats
folded under our heads. Or the thought
that our coats may be gone in the morning,
or the fleas jumping from the straw
on the floor.

Child Setting the Table for Breakfast

It was before morning, before anyone was up,
a raw wing brushed him—the child
setting foot in the cave of pantry,
a light-cord hovering just out of reach,
a stool shaking under him like a trestle
as he climbed, dragged the plates down
one by one, odd and bitter
in their embattled porcelain.
He was setting the table for his mother
still dreaming under moony folds of linen—
how could she know what it was like?
He had promised, he could not move.
Where was voice, bird?
The clock had no face, outdoors
trees leaned on each other
in a night sweat too thick to dislodge.
He saw how it was. No guarantee the world
could turn on its big hinge frosted with terror—
space beyond space where the sun might be falling
even now, in the wrong direction.
He whimpered like a lonely animal
smelling the death of the planet,
nuzzled the window pane beside him, breathing,
breathing until a clear patch widened.
From the spark of himself, rubbed life,
enough to climb down from the stool, take
knives and forks from the depths of a cabinet,
lay them on the stunned table.
Just as a grey lip parted over the lawn,
he went to the foot of the stairs and called her.

To the Orphans

The angel of childhood looks across two wars
without thinking. How did he know
exactly what it would be like?
Stronger than we are, the child
looked into the pool of adult loneliness,
saw a penetrable sorrow, a mirage flickering.
If we look back straight, which is not the same
as remembering, we will be grafted again,
closer, on this six-day world—
like the orphans we liked best in first grade,
filing into school in outgrown clothes,
with chapped hands, that odd odor of abandonment.
Their eyes were indifferent to teachers.
On summer afternoons when the steamy day
almost stopped, they went first into the marsh
by the playground, hunting the fiercest secrets,
trailing their feet in a black pond which appalled us.
It was they who turned over the dead rabbit,
stroked its slick side half-opened by maggots.
Now in a cramp of history, in the smoke of
the deaths of children, we think of the orphans,
those princes who preferred being frogs,
unafraid in the shadows of the school basement,
the galvanized crash of thunder.
What could lightning do,
which had already severed everything?
They knew they would always be found on another
doorstep.

Carnival

As children we were afraid of carnivals, especially
the sideshows, which we were not allowed to enter.
Seeing, nevertheless, shadows
jerk on the soiled tent flap, smelling unhappy flesh
violated by something we did not know.
Of death we were afraid with a greater fear,
the limbs of a pet rabbit contracting
bitterly on the grass.
We have since been instructed in these things,
no longer so curious. Though sometimes we get up early
to look in the grass for our first, delicate sorrow,
and sometimes we're lucky, climbing the stairs to bed,
feeling something wrong, like a bird in the house,
falling asleep to dream of carnivals.
Musky canvas slips over us.
The fat lady smiles from her moon of flesh,
she has always known that we loved her,
the dwarf steadies his head, a big lantern,
over his ghostly patch of earth.
He is not afraid, neither are we. Though
we will never get used to the world, never—
over a moonlit trestle, a train rocks out of town
each dawn, faces of carnival pressed to the window.
They seem to be cheering us on, watching us
work into our shadows, sprouting a hump,
a good third limb, kept retracted all this time.

Coming Out of the Movies

As a child I suffered a kind of terror
coming out of the intense white life of movies,
and used to prepare for it by imagining,
before I even got out of the dark lobby—
entering the living room at home
where nothing ever really happened;
where the curtains had hung the same old roses
for years, and my mother moved
steadily between sideboard and kitchen.

A lie, of course. We
are forced to imagine our certainties
from the beginning, our parents conspiring
as they can, banking their accumulated fire.
It's a terrible thing to be an adult.
We never make it, of course,
to adulthood I mean—
and it's the same now,
raising my swimming head from a book,
trying to re-imagine the room I'm in—
the oak table I bought for its stability,
my grandmother's German silver teapot
dented with use. I never use it, and
I'm still choking in Dostoevski's brown fire,
the tight rooms of a house in St. Petersburg,
life brought to a pitch.

Worse still, if I told the truth, is the fact
that I'm always reading now, compulsively,
unable to stop, things coming to this pitch.
What I'm reading is my thick life
which piled up before I could think.
I can hardly breathe among the terrors, the ardors,
the figments of my green life.
No movie comes close to it.

Seeing

A mystical business, this thing of the houses
we live in, collect by painful accretion,
growing one on top of another, until we
travel in all our houses at once, each
tilting inside the last,
a top-heavy, helpless crustacean.
And at the pearled, mucousy center, the
tiny, shocked membrane of the eye vibrating
with self-induced light, absorbing everything,
giving it back,
a cosmos of irritable color—

It begins, a thicket of maternal odors. The child
nosing into a bureau drawer, pushing up
garments, wild, personal. Twists
with the speed of light, he doesn't know how,
and he sees for the first time, in a
silent explosion. His vision skids
along pear-colored boards, a floor, he
doesn't know where, shoots off in parallel lines
to the wind-struck clapboards of a house in Michigan,
where the leathery pods of a locust tree
must be clicking even now.

The boards were grey. He
remembers the rattle of the locust outside
his window, the scratching of lizards
on the roof of a sunbaked adobe in Arizona.
The sun clanged, he looked into it, discovered
another eye, always open,
a lizard on the powdered terrace, extending
one leg with infinite patience, with the

slowness of centuries. How explain the way
its scales stretched in the act, the way a window
once, in a Bronx apartment,
turned blue with all possible grief.

Even now, things are entering the jelly of my eye,
their homely constellations: they
stay, quiver,
and we are wrecked on the eye's infinities.
No one dies—
If anyone ever died, the cities would collapse
into a murky hotel, into the suppurating dust
that blows from the stiff-armed galaxies
which could not twang, amber,
wheel, except beading up on our
original strings. Think of everything collapsing at once
in the corner of a Bronx apartment.

For Luke Moore

The child who died did not have much to say,
flung back, in his parcel of breath—
crossed over, crossed over
the dark, trembling lathes.
Where did he look,
Giant-step?
I dreamt I woke up in the wrong sleeve,
a sour linen, tasting of time.

It's difficult, crows marching
four abreast down the highway
far as the eye can see.
Who flies this rag on its pole?
A love, nailed to the hill,
taking the long way round,
collecting children like burdocks
by swamp light.

There is nothing warm, decorous, delicate.
The river, in full flood, has
deposited coffins in the tops of trees.
Give him back, among the cracks, the
tense dirt—swinging at the end of our lines,
awake all over, still rubbed with our smell.
Between the break-neck roots,
literal trees,
nails, leather, string,
give him back, terrible one.

Photograph Album

Child, the book says, child,
make friends with the uncanny light
which your relatives lived in, dipped in their
textures: a ribbon fluttering by the white fence,
a hat stepping into a boat, picnics
always spread between.
Their starch held up through betrayals.
If they went limp on thundery afternoons,
they said nothing, retiring to their bedrooms,
the air cracking over the houses, like tough silk.

They grew flowers, funny things—
lemonbalm, boxwood, verbena,
the back yards lacing into thick greenhouses.
Perhaps at the end of a long day
aching with discreet silence,
a bead of desire formed on the great fern,
sprinklers assailed their ears with humming stars.

We walk into their night packed with candelabra,
sighing with knowledge, theirs and ours.
Who talk too much, still wanting to be happy,
having failed again, being human.

Driving Home in Winter

Something glows over the dwindling century,
not political. I fear it, driving home
through the cold, New England mountains,
the face of my mother who is dead,
swimming toward me along the highway.
She ran away once in her senility,
down a Vermont road, catching on bird scar
in the stumbly woods, looking for another
country. There is snow and trembling,
my mother leaning, muttering, trying to
make out her face in the smoky spoon of the world.

A silo stations itself in black wind, pours
twilight as I pass, over the uncanny fields.
Home is a long way, I don't know how
I will get there; the first idiom extinguished,
the winds hoarse with eternity, inventing
this long mother who runs beside me.
What was she saying all those years?
The hills don't know, folding back
brown, silver, like old valises,
and I don't stop anywhere to think, the road
hurling itself steadily toward a low star.

Farewell to the Body

We try to think about it but find
that impossible, suspended in its smoke
and water—leaching to two small windows,
cloudy at best, twitching in their silver jelly
like fish. Through which we wink, send a
love beam—and my eye
falls on the tree, in a burst of applause,
under which you stand.
Come closer. I see you
pressed to the pane, which melts,
whereupon you enter, all sparks and pearwood,
and speak,
which can't be exactly recorded. Meanwhile
the tree, a burst of invisible leaves,
scratches on the tinfoil of the retina,
scratches in a perfect cornucopia,
emblazoned, etched, mottled, quivering,
transparent to the last green flaw.
The colors drip into your bones. Not
into your brain waving far up on its stalk,
but into the chalk and salt of your bones,
that barrow, ancient, porous, serious,
fresh beyond all argument.

*

Something sad, something sacred about the body
from which all arguments rise. Once
I left a peach on the kitchen counter for a week,
watching the transformations: the way it
teemed, sank, soaked toward center—grew a blue
powder all over, then a black, dense, velvety—
then collapsed into a kind of bud
or navel turned inside out. Then leaked all its juice

forever, in a sticky trail on the formica.
—Maybe this was blasphemous, but I
thought about my mother's body
slipped into the ground in Vermont
six years earlier, and wondered if by now
it looked like the peach. If it
had soaked up all the mud and gravel,
poured out of itself in a long, forgetful tongue;
become a sluice, a runnel, a cycle
of vapors, sunk into a silvery
coalseam or underground river.

*

Sacred. I remember reading how Marie Curie
kissed the bits of her husband's brain
given to her after he died
in an accident. I thought it morbid at the time
but can't now—coming closer to the noise
my bones make, grinding, slowly pulverizing
their red sockets. I thank them
for keeping going, and the curious gristle
that keeps me warm, these wrappings, cerements,
vellum, whatever—
the blue hills of my veins pumping harder
every day, mapping into extravaganzas—
countries, constellations, splotched, ardent,
the spatterings of a whole erratic lifetime.
An annotated text beginning to curl and ruffle,
rolling up the pleasures of one erratic, ecstatic lifetime;
a prick song for the invisible
which will have to be played out in another story.

*

In the brown depths of the groin, a groan, a burl
of fire licking at the stomach—the whole scaffold,
beyond a doubt, beginning to mutter in the wind.
Yet climbing the old staircase, looking out
again from the turret, I receive an arrow
in the eye. A sparrow lights
in my ribcase, whistles in the gap,
and I understand that this is my body,
the one window I can't look in at, the sputtering linen
I bed down in every night, a horn of breath
furling the dark leaves of my nostrils.
And how can I bed down anywhere else,
sow the black seed of myself, except in
this sack, this sock of juices, these bowels
intricately contrived, miles and miles
of incandescent plumbing. How squeak
in any other language, than the body's
thick, beloved gutturals.

I thank the whole miraculous, tireless
contraption, which may tire of me soon,
which I imagine now, swimming in its final colors,
the color of fish and smoke.
Which I try to despatch with, stamp off
like a snow loaf, the warm crumbs
still clinging to my naked legs,
walking away forever,
one side dry.

II

What Matters

In Paradise, nothing came between
the eye and the tree.
Our first face was bland, set
with a milky, parental eye
which nevertheless begot on the bland moon
ditches full of sharp children,
the fathers of wars, tearing their beards,
displacing our eyes with tears.

Summer night, laced with the smell of childbed,
women rubbing themselves like snails
over oblivious walls.
The tree hums with dark traffic,
they do not listen. What matters
is to stand up each morning,
hang up the wash stiff with mistakes,
not reject the terrible years.

Angel

Sometimes a man makes an angel
out of his bright confusion, clothes it,
sets it in the middle of things.
The hedgerows play pitch and toss,
the breath of the unborn blows over,
blackbirds take off like smoke
in the terrible light of the ordinary.

We rise, enter the world, equivocations greening.
How is it you count every face
without arriving at scorn?
Children swarm out of the schoolyard,
their hearts clap like hornbooks,
they know what they know.
We greet them in the light, the shade,
an old board full of nails and dew.

Speak,
say what you are, brooding
in painful complicity.
A long sunset begins, a red trestle
thrown over the dark machines.

Braque Said

All things reverberate, said Braque, and they do.
Some tormented, like spoons by salt, windows by
light whose harsh sail cracks and darkens in an instant.
We are these thick selves trying, these opaque vessels,
though sometimes our mouths fill with light,
saying a few words over, giving
a reading of things as if we knew them.
We do not know them, so something stitches
the unsteady cloth, scours the eye to perceive
moon, starling, leaves — faces
jewelled with distinct shadow, turning
hour by hour through their windless abrasions.
Light-pummelled, light-obedient we will go down,
astonished to the end by the vision striking the window,
though it's only the kitchen garden again, cabbages
creeping their rows like big, thoughtful snails;
and it's only another day to traverse together,
collecting in sporadic dews of attention, vibrating
to the old stories, spoons listening from
the kitchen table. As one grows older
life and art become one, Braque said.

Among the Paintings of Andrew Wyeth

The crow is dead and black, the fish is dead
on the white beach, snow hisses in shocks
of dry corn hung from rafters. And faces keep watch,
embedded in the grains of a silence—
Tom Clark, Willard Snowden, Allen Lynch,
spell upon spell.
The earth seems homesick for them, though they
are there, half-sunk in its shadow,
half-looking into porchless light.
Rather, half turned for the painter
whom they barely notice, so slow his hand,
so slow the wheel of his vision,
his cloth becoming their cloth.
A strip of gingham, forgotten on a line,
blows into nothing on the sea wind, and
the things we neglect, persist, casting
the longest shadows. Like our faces
in their baffled disrepair. Like Wyeth's millgate,
frozen in service, still clinging to an empty dam.
Clamped to ourselves, rusting, silvering,
we fill up with our quota of darkness, spill
over in the homeless dusk. Not lonely
among Wyeth's true, bleached fields,
the grey houses emptied of themselves.
Alvaro, Christina, gone through their plain, wood doors.

Van Gogh

We are like this, in every particular,
green trying to become blue. A man
shovelling, a man eating and weeping,
leaning forward in his chair.
The edges of his flesh curl
like a thick, private page.
It is necessary to eat and weep,
because the light uses up everything,
flying back, in a rain of mallets—
as if a man should contract a fever
which does not dispel,
maintaining itself in the charred log.
We gather around the supper.
Black bread, black soup, potatoes
blowing ashes in our eyes.
The chair gnaws a hole in the floor,
with its stubby, yellow root.

*

Behind the asylum at St. Remy,
the Lord is angry. The wheat field mounts,
boils like the molten hay of heaven,
breaks and stays.
And now my life begins, under a poultice
clapped over the left side of my face
which is green and melting. I
will rake the stubble behind this heavy house
where the windows slam open, offending me.
That bench in the corner is lonelier than Christ.

Lord, you lit these ligaments,
make me the thing of terror which you made,
phosphoring through all the layers.
Watch,
I will make the sun stop on a hill,
the rock expel a tongue of cypress,
then a ruck of constellations,
cantering, milk of gold!
You have not seen such things.
You have never made a blue like the blue
I made in the lake behind the fields at St. Remy.

Museums and Fevers

We should leave ourselves frequently, in
a longer movement, for the cool wings
of a museum or theatre
where other fevers divide in a patch of umber.
Though this is only a foretaste
shaped with infinite speed and patience
in the thick rains of a man's spirit—
his mud, his solitudes decanted
in hunger, decanted again in thirst.

Redwinged blackbirds skirl in snow.
Outside it is March, the garden even now
laced with irretrievable crocus.
Pray that we may be delivered from the
wrong mirrors, citizens of a broken vision
richer than we can explain—the syntax
still romantic,
a box of astrological instruments
glowing faintly in the dark.

Bird in the armory, repeat. The hospitals
are overflowing, their blood runs down
the street, in nine disaffected colors
past the museum walls.
We are looking at another picture.
A cloud swims up over blue woods,
children file through a yellow gate.
In this silence stocked with cries,
to name is an act of love.

Inexhaustible, do not call yourself
in question. God putters and sighs, a
Sunday pensioner, dispels our darkness
like a possible road. Perhaps
at the last moment, we will
dissolve in a good sheet of tears,
approaching that corner of the garden
where pictures efface themselves, all
the bird cages empty, inconsolable with song.

In Gratitude to Pissaro for His Woman and Child at the Well

It is real noon in the picture by Pissaro.
We did not know how grey we were, how tired
until we looked, unspooled in the light nets
of the painter—the thatched greens and
wickets of the little orchard, the patch
of pink, trowelled earth behind it.
A watering can tips where it was dropped,
seems to dream in its improvised texture.
The woman leans in a forgetful space, propped
by substantial folds of apron, her
hand falling open in a fine, cool gesture.

Then uncurl.
Having come so far, with so much effort,
discover what really matters—that is,
moss, and Pissaro's red-tiled roofs
absorbing their spatter of color over and over.
Here are runnels, pooled and blue,
the bricks of an old well.
Pissaro's trees collect sun and hold.

The Beautiful Estrangements

No life has ever suited me so well
as this one, the very one I'm in. The
mulled grey air of classrooms, offices,
comforting somehow. Like the fog
that rolls across a mountain road
when you're driving somewhere,
making it impossible to look down or back
into the terrifying valleys.
And there's nothing ahead but road, climbing
all by itself, carrying the car up with it,
preoccupied with the act of climbing, by the next stone
glassed in mist, the hooded tree
at the turn, sunk deep in its own mysterious life.
Which nevertheless, bows slightly
at your passing.

It's lonely. I suppose you could
call it lonely. Except that the world
presses close to the opaque windows, and
you begin seeing things, one by one,
against the fog—the worst moments
of your life.
Like the day your mother pushed you away
after your father died, angry that you
were still there, and he wasn't. Or
entering the big, waxed bell of a ballroom

for your first lesson in formal dancing,
the red, angry faces of children lining the walls.

And always, of course, those moments you can't
abide, when you have to get out of yourself
like a stuffy, downtown movie house.
When everything you've thought and done
slides by like a stale, erotic film
you've been forced to watch for centuries.
Still we're never ourselves, not nearly,
and I like the smell of downtown movie houses,
the dry popcorn, the musky and desperate teenagers—
such places have begun to shine.
As if I'd fallen in love with each lost day,
knowing I'm always travelling up in my patch of fog,
appearances sometimes otherwise.
I don't know who or what it is,
working these beautiful estrangements.

Evening Enjambed with Sparrows

This is the world, we say, seating ourselves
in a low chair by the window, the street light
drawing flotillas of shadows—
they are fish or lemons. Desire
is a primary color, the man with no luck
who hugs his life close like a parcel of razors.
We watch him wandering home through the alley,
in full heat. He curses the moon's white chunk.
Nothing more ordinary than the way
he drifts in and out of our vision.

Evening, a solitary work enjambed with sparrows,
birds with modest vocabularies—and
we are reading the book of extinct animals,
travelling backward on their exhausted breath
until we can hardly see them anymore.
They are there, under the streets, swimming
inside us as we crest, our neighbors lashed to our sides,
the bricks, the houses, the planet itself, lining itself
with our stories—at the center of this speed,
making a pact with gravity.

If the city scratches, and we have not understood
after all, your wrists blue as delphinium
come and go, the barefooted stones of the alley
come and go, the drunk man spins home,
still happy in his bright immersion.
He lodges in the drifting window,
the steeple whittles another hole in the fog.
By the least touch of earth we know, rain
arriving in a steady moment—there is nothing,
nothing except this fragrant hammering.

These Days

The dead need no rest, they walk through the rain
carrying the town on their backs.
We pretend not to notice, though
the sky thickens with their names,
and evenings they crack a whip
down the length of the saffron street.
Another spasm of history, don't try to sleep.
They're shooting again outside the hotel.

How slowly dust collects in the bottoms of pans.
Your lover dislodges from your side, afraid
because the guns have stopped, only
beetles twittering in the old garden.
You let him go because it doesn't matter,
your ears rumbling with transcendent weather;
nor shall you try again, year after year,
to thread yourself on the roots of his stale guitar.

Rejoice, a sun loaf breaks at the window,
and they are still there, the dead,
the unborn fretting in their sleeves,
raising the hammer, morning,
bringing it down.
You hang up the wash another time, happy now,
almost forfeit—having saved
everything against the occasion.

Crows are Impossible in Heaven

Franz Kafka

Crows are impossible in heaven
though one crow is watching the sky hang up sheets,
like a dead thing,
Civitas Dei, a crow on his twig:
one branch, another, two crows
squatting in wet weather, catching
each other's eye.
They speak: we are our own medium,
two liquids travelling in the same direction,
our blue gristle moving toward consummation
beyond the drafty nebulae—
servants of the horse, the man,
who ride off into their empty vibration
over the earth which does not know them.

It is wet, two crows take an oath of office.
Two justified crows hitch themselves
onto the spine of a limber wind, ride off
over four hooves, transparent, frightening
the bystanders with their hoarse love,
the poverty, the rust of their twin cry.
Jubilato.
Day after the last, without anything changing,
they arrive in the kingdom.
Their hearse is not cracked stone.
Scholars of dirt, they will not be swept,
a final leaving, through the jointless broom.

Citizens, rising, cawing with devotion,
filling the stadium with blurred voices,

they did not study how to die,
their red coal stamped with the fern of desire.
The city forms, latent with power,
the sun drops out of their black, stuffed groins.

In a Corner of Toulouse Lautrec

The color of flesh, we are made aware of,
is blue as a zinc hip bath
in the corner of a painting called *La Toilette.*
Other flesh is amber, ochre,
dropsical over a silvery, middle-aged rump—
a pucker of tallow at the corner of the mouth.
How we foul ourselves, dew the cloth
of this promenade, as if somewhere else
we might be rewrapped. Not here,
not under the lamps of the Moulin Rouge,
dripping green from their sputtery gas jets
into our upturned faces, our pores warming
to a froth. M. Boileau warms
to his evening, leans across the table,
pins the waitress, with a yellow eye.

To see is everything. The eye
that does not violate but saturates,
purging itself in an absinthe glare. So color
absolves us, so we become pure color
at the end, swimming in a vein of Toulouse Lautrec.
These apparitions of staleness and ardor. This
humid, dissolving, spangled.

III

Room by Moonlight

In a saving smell of bedclothes, the moon
collects, fire shirt
at the window: our search develops
in this direction. What are deaths?
There is only this road leading from
the thought of you, emerging like a clarity
at my elbow, nor is there anything like
our salt.

Music has porches, pitched this way
from cadence to cadence—what
you took up when you lifted me
thus far. I address myself to your hands
as we redden, you ascend my spine,
the bedclothes thump, all the
hampers in the land responding;
we allow ourselves space to rain

in our skin which leans like a bush
from the crevice of our departures.
Don't move, the door will open, a sentence
slip through, perfecting itself,
threatening us with dazzling coherencies
in the room where we have just been born.
Sleep, it's what we came for,
the juices drying on our foreheads,
riding, riding until morning,
your shoulder which bumps and stays.
This is the moon, a thin tunic,
white enough by most standards
to do justice to our eyes, their defections,
our bodies opening like bewildered cliffs,
grappling, unsteady with candor.

Come Brother

One wants to be loved, here and
at all times, in this room where
we sleep on our long-stemmed shadows,
generating along several lines.
Form and desire says the world,
rising, drawing over our bellies
its harsh and lasting silk.

But it's you one wants to be loved by,
to love in the desperate
inventions of the flesh,
in a space too intense for speech
on hot mornings when the traffic slows.
We are still tangent, clipping from
an angle like wary scissors.

Come brother, lover, beached here,
becoming almost legible. Jointly
we define an orbit that sputters
back to the beginning, children
in our towering choices.
Even God is answerable in the coarse
bush of the spirit. He stands,

a man famous for silences, among
the privies and the fishhouses,
light striking one side of his face.
We have worn out our obsessions,
tested our powers of transfiguration,
and the air now, off the balcony, bluer than sea,
crashes through the imaginary shutters.

Suburbs

There's only one solitude, its profound laws, and
we're mistaken about the temperature of the sun. It's
snowing everywhere at once in the precincts of the brown city.
We listen for the solitary walker, the blown cape
of his mind. The earth, a tiny bitter citadel
falls through his lonely fire.
Then prophesy. Berries stand at the edge of winter,
already ripe with cold. A woman at an iced window
has rubbed a place to look through.
We prophesy,
milling in a fine dance of introspection, space
mingling with space until it seems like nothing,
the blizzard at the window, its ornate cloud, its
tired devices.
The suburban skies fall up, night
dusts all the beautiful porches.
We rock over the sills of our solitary rooms.

The Rose Arriving

Pure rumor, the light in the room,
white, declarative at the edges,
the piano a rainy silence. We
do not listen, this stretch of
pale language will soon be over.
The table confronts us, legs tooled like burdocks,
round, rough, thorough. We redden
by virtue. The experience arrives
on our tongues, a bitter vernacular.

There is no evidence, there is no crime.
Though we have failed as anecdote, light
continues to pour from the ceiling,
the table edges into the wind,
chanting in each particular. We
are nourished by many bodies, their
transparent storms. The rose
arriving suddenly, ahead
of the thin forsythia, at the pane.

This Place

The best thing about this place
is the rain. The appearance
of morning every morning,
one cloud standing over.
Old house, all corners, there is about you
a smell of earth, a delicate storm
in the curtains at all times.
And we like the cry of the dustman
from street to street. The way
he seems to turn in at the gate,
mount the stairs.

Nothing holds like the body, this
tough stuff we tell ourselves
we are not made of.
Stir and sigh, another afternoon
which can never be cancelled,
crickets, grass, the sea—a dark wax
pacifying itself.
Trees, which know nothing of us,
build another cone of fragrance.
These gestures of pleasure
keep rising.

Such Afternoons

What is there to talk about, except the earth,
its ancient freshness, grass sputtering
with children and new graves. Also
beetles so top-heavy, so drugged with thought,
they tip over trying to navigate the simplest distance.
Though it's only one day after another, never
the day we're after, though we walk
the pear-shaped earth in gravely wounded lives,
such afternoons arrive. A fine languor of cicada,
my neighbor peering into his hedges
like an earnest bird. What does he see there?
Something good, I think.
It's possible to stop worrying the dark for a while,
following the chirp of an old lawnmower
chewing its ragged way around the lawn.
Our feet moving without effort,
their depressions filling with quiet water.

NOVEMBER

The issue of a private bargain, we pass from
night into morning, address each other
by first light—a threadbox of rain and snow
unravelling down the driveway.
We feel strange to ourselves. It's
almost the end of the century, and
the old are not mad enough, neither are we.
Unprepared for the great silence,
the little ones before it.

It's always like this in November, standing
by the front window, looking out
at the oak on the lawn
injected with the color of our thought,
a bit of snow on everything.
The house is under the sky,
and everything has a claim on us,
even the spaces between things,
a set of tracks filling up behind us.

Still we go on rehearsing, revising
the blue charts of childhood, which
are rapidly turning into smoke,
and November seems to go on forever.
We arrive again each morning,
touch, speak,
agree to the taste of the day. Sit down
by the kitchen stove, our clothes
smelling wet and black, like travellers.

March

Wet tree, green stone. Coupling of starlings
in the shrill cloud, falling for a moment
through windy light.
Hard to rejoice, even so, and the moment
thickens. Starlings beat back, straw
in their bills, the pressure resumes
inside stones.
A voice, high, panicky,
rising from the new grass.

What shall we say, rising fat, ruddy,
inarticulate from last night's dreams?
That a starling is breaking up the neighborhoods,
that our terrors repeat themselves at midnight,
their simple vibrations—
These solitudes beget themselves
on the quick stuff of the world.

Hanging Loose

Rereading each other from all sides, as if
we were not already perfect strangers, we tilt
to the lateral sun, a series of disappointing surfaces.
Yet looking is a kind of love, and your forehead
branches with a vine or river.
It quivers,
tree of your thought, your disposition,
disappears around the corners of your skull
becoming again mere compost,
white char dug up in a midden.
So we delve,
so the spider drums at his post.
So we draw things off, their savor,
through a discrete ventricle.

In the beginning was water, the back yard,
chips of a broken walk
down which the child hopped like a grackle,
glossy-shouldered, shaking off the steady rain.
Oh, it was fine!
Everything packed together like a close jewel,
your face dipping in and out of the leaves,
honeycombed, pierced by shadow.

We freshen, in a perspiration called time, falling
faster than anything, in love with the trees.
They move off lightly. Stay delicate then
and loose, until the day your heart crashes,
blind, seismic.

Watercolor

We are working on a watercolor of our condition.
The barracks badly lit, potatoes
spreading an onion-like sadness
from the back of the oil stove.
Voices die at this altitude, though
sometimes we hear other things.
A rat blundering behind a grey section,
a piece of hemp walking the floor.

How do we live? That's not the question.
Only one man keeps going,
rubbing down the boards, shaking out the bunks.
In the sleeves of an ordeal, we might do something.
If it were war or winter, horses pounding
toward the red barberry. Or
summer, the magicians dangling by their heels,
bleeding in different colors.

We are not naked enough, small enough
to make an exit. The poor build their coffins
at noon, out of fresh air,
planks of disaster, never
doubting that death wants them.
Their cry does not come to us—
the tundra pressed against the window
like a flat slipper.

We hover, our detachment becoming
almost radiant. Someone

is scrubbing potatoes
in a stiff cloud the color of lard.
A plate sticks to the table, a lavender beetle
is crossing it.
We dip the sponge in the bucket,
draw it over the picture.

Crowed Up

Meditation was not enough, the table of universals
spread out again on cheap cloth,
book, biscuit, sewing machine.
Nothing moved, welling like intelligence,
the vestibule smelling of dogs and umbrellas.
He rummaged.
The moon rose behind the kitchen shelf,
an old plate criss-crossed with reflections,
the spokes of a shadow seemed to touch him.

Faces fell from his fingers, in brown chalk.
How many impressions had he taken, the house
of his sensibility shifting, leaves brushing,
smoking behind him,
the cicada repeating its dry verb.
The world buckled like world at the window,
an unsteady coal, losing outline.
The gas meter ticked,
sustaining the penny of his winter.

At the gates of heaven, he would try again,
reassembling the sewing machine,
stitching his song in a night of insects.
What deeper than their crackling,
the nerves in a carapace of fire,
stitching the tragic grass of summer evening,
long grass, silk of his understanding.
Surely the grackle sun will crack its beak
for him in his cloven place.

He makes no arrangements among the gravel,
the bug-riddled foliage. His meditation burnishes

though he is no meditator,
a cricket established in homely fire.
The gates crow him up, the netted
metal cock crows him up.
It is not mercy,
his hammer was not patience.

IV

October

We live in great commotions, reminded
in advance, a note left on the front steps,
quarried in hurried fire.
The old woman at the end of the street
sweeps herself into a bronze ambush,
disappears,
leaving behind an archaic fan of broom tracks.

It could scare you, stroke
of the back yards laid open
word by word, the strong trees
beginning to gallop.
The hedges clap in a stitch
they do not understand, split
along the yoke, drop everything
at once, like a tragic wardrobe.

October, old pestle, compounding us
with our shadows, the neighborhoods
gorged with light, crack,
discharge their squibs,
the years, unremarkable, carried off
in thick vegetable smoke.
What shall we make of the trees
pricked into dark camphor, hanging
by their perfect wrists?
We finish our journals quickly, press
them onto the heap, trickling a thread
of color, take to the sidewalks.

Much is discarded. The worlds thump
like empty warehouses, birds
pour from an invisible crease.
We dream our way, something at heart
unidentified, entering the vestibule of the cold.
Walking west, due west,
growing amber, thinner.

Near Cortland, NY

Today when I woke up, I didn't know
where I was. And once I admitted
that to myself, no one else around
at the time, the huge, nerveless pain
of being locked in this one, stupid life forever,
lifted and went off through the ceiling.
And a landscape I saw only once,
near Cortland, New York, moved into
the sea space left, complete in every detail.
A pale, soaked plain of corn in early March.
Tall rows of bleached stalks
turning to each other, brushing, whispering
in a kind of curious dance.

I don't know why that corn was never cut
but I saw it clearly from the car window—
stooping, beckoning in the raw March wind.
A scarecrow harvest birds would never seek,
a strange, standing, useless grain.
I liked it so much I didn't ask myself why,
nor do I now—
or equally, the lank, yellow hills
standing up around like a dull triptych.
Just two ranks of low, yellow hills,
a corn field tucked in between.

I like to keep the door open
to places like that. They keep invading
my thoughts, but clearly aren't mine,
though something of my grandmother
hovered over the field. Not her face
exactly, but an old, rosewood melodeon
which stood unused in her parlor for years,
stuck on one quavering note.
As children, we kept pressing that one yellow key,
the only one left that still gave off a sound.
It climbed and complained, kept complaining.
It filled the air.

What I Have to Say About Death

We're lucky there's so much space between things.
Between birth and death, one word
and the next. Between your last remark
and the long silence that followed.
I hadn't seen my mother for years
before she died. So
it doesn't seem as if she had died—
only gone away again, to the west coast
or somewhere.
We'll see each other again.

Spaces take up most of the room.
It used to upset me as a child
that the sparrow at the winter window,
feathering there suddenly, brown pulse
in all that vertiginous white,
wouldn't stay and talk for a while.
It knew better
and flicked away, bird-like, into
the staring geometries. As if
the whole world were nothing anyhow
but an explosion of incomprehensible light.

It's always like that, even with love
which is only a noun, after all,
for a series of incomparable moments.
Like the face of your son caught by camera
in his tenth year. Sun striking his
suddenly emerging face—sharp, lonely,
already turning in its singular direction.
Or the texture of your husband's sleeve

as he leaned on the breakfast table one morning.
He was saying something he really meant,
blue, fresh, like the stuff of his shirt.
It never got better after that.

We would like to give full devotion
to everything around us. But
nothing stays long enough, weaving away
in an erratic dance. Our names
disappearing even as we say them.
Our name is desire, if anything,
clinging as we do, with all our might,
to what escapes us,
burning among the beautiful absences.
A sparrow hits the window lightly,
bounces off, a bead of shot.
Which is what I have to say about death.

Starling

All things ride toward extinction,
and I never knew it better than this morning.
Grey stone of a terrible morning,
carved, cursed, delivered
with blessings into my open hands.
A week in which nothing passed.
No work lit by love or imagination,
no thought lit by love or imagination.

Next came the terrible idea, that
maybe I'd never been true to anything,
any word, any deed—and my will
came to a dead stop. All the hammers
suspended, kicking in air,
the whole machine quivering with shock.
Then it happened. A starling
flopped down on the porch right in front of me,
split its yellow beak, said what a starling always does—
Creak, like a rusty hinge,
said it again.

I have always liked those birds, starlings.
Dirty, stubby tailed pests as they are,
without distinction or song, there's
something magnificent about them.
Something that says I'm here
whether anyone wants me or not.
And they're here all right, everywhere, the starlings.
My neighbors go after them with guns.

After that, I threw this morning after all the others,
a pebble I mistook for a boulder.
Let my words sink back into the ground.

Homing

We keep arranging things for a last inspection
as if they were indispensable. The house, one side
veining with moss, the loose stone of the doorstep,
retilted after every winter; the blue panes
of the living room windows, rubbed deeper
with each child's going. The children call back,
they are fine. The maple in the front yard,
pruned from a sapling, has developed three gold elbows,
drops thicker leaves every fall.

We keep homing as if we didn't know
that the tree can't be interested forever.
Though it tries, and somehow we feel etched,
at least roughed out in shadow, on its wooden heart.
Hard to admit
that we're plunging in another direction,
a loose debris of love and recollection,
a dark straw tangled with darker intentions.
The tree is indispensable.

Ebb

An ebb falls,
amber without weather,
when what we see without seeing,
becomes this purifying reach.
Afloat on our infirmities, we
turn over, green and stem,
in the irony which makes love possible,
find in unstable day
a musical equivalence.
This is what we are given,
our fair share,
blue bite of spirit,
river becoming bridge,
sea becoming shore,
everything drawn along.
Even the ambitious griefs
still hard at work,
tying, retying
their aimless, self-absorbed knots.

Imagining Freedom

It's too bad one has to imagine it. And
it's impossible of course, to imagine
something one has never seen.
But I know what it's like,
freedom.
It's like a mountain village called Casares
where I have never been.
But I have a photograph of it on my desk—
a tiny white village strewn down the reddish rock
of an impossibly old mountain in Spain.
Like an outcropping of the mountain itself,
pressed that hard into the earth
by a sky of such solid light
that the mountain has to press back again.
I look at the snapshot often, aware
of something I can't quite see, the light
in the picture is so intense.
It's there, nevertheless,
a shadow.
Maybe the sense of days and days
spent in a place I can't really love
though I try to. Afraid
I'm the place I can't really love.
As if the wrong rock,
black, vitreous, volcanic,
had deposited itself in my chest, and I

couldn't press back hard enough to dislodge it.
Maybe so,
I let it stay.
Every mountain must have absorbed
a piece of bad rock in its day. The early
days, turbulent days of its making,
which is still there like a splinter
which no longer hurts. Become part
of the complex heart it's embedded in.

When you're not busy doing something else,
think of Casares,
its porous, half-demolished walls
where as many birds live as people.
Where centuries of living, which are also suffering,
have soaked into the stones and ceased to be suffering,
become weeds and goats and sun without stint
pouring through the crooked houses,
holding them up.
That's freedom—to outlast yourself
and find yourself still there, only happier,
cemented by an ancient light
that knows a lot more than you do.
Knocking at a small wooden door in the Costa del Sol,
entering while you're still knocking.

City

The sun rises early and late, and we know
what it's like to stop in the middle of the street,
factories opening their exhausted wings.
Metal smoke, cruelty,
the wheel dipping into its own blood,
and something else we don't understand—
our meditations have always been violent.
An organ grinder forms like a bead on the far corner,
grinding out another city,
tiny and rainy.

Love collects in the foreground,
an old man on a park bench, set into
his life absorbing him drop by drop,
the frame gilding.
We would like to beg his pardon for everything,
yet hasn't he been happy, haven't we,
inserted into this place we cannot change?
A tree catches wind in the black courtyard.
We watch it, meaning what we mean,
inhabiting ourselves like a cracked, sufficient word.

Reader

Seen from another angle, we are less ridiculous.
Here is a book, a bed, someone
propped on his elbow,
reading through the aching night
as if his eyes were a hundred years old.

The closet is hale with moths, light-
years draw away. Yet he reads,
obsessive nerve, reads with
his unhappy blood
at the doors of the world,
harries the sour hotel of the dead.
The bramble of his wives, his jobs
taking fire from black words.
Towards dawn he begins to burn on his own,
a thicket embossed with much suffering.

Let God reconsider.
Though we're not kind or clever,
wheeling, dealing in these scandalous bodies,
there's a bird up our sleeve,
everything is as we say.

ALMOST GREEK

The languages arrange themselves again,
all the harrowing explanations, leaving
things pretty much the same,
donkeys braying in the old garden,
poplars drawing together at noon,
each a delicate tooth of shade.
We are attached to this handkerchief of exile,
exactly the size of our imaginations,
the eye of a needle which we walk through
unattended—
almost Greek.

Here then, our limp is not noticeable,
pearled by steady light from the sea,
which hums through the dark cinemas,
their stale protocols of death.
The old do not notice,
burning up slowly in their patch of history,
not afraid—since events are always fatal—
being born, for instance,
trodden out in the coarse sheets.
Sun stokes their hearts to the end,
who pick up each moment as it falls.

Poem of Gratitude

A bead has formed at the very tip of my life.
Or what seems like the tip of my life,
from this vantage. Though
the tree may still be extending itself
way up there—the sun is generous.
I know this by a peculiar happiness
running through each leafy day. By
the fact that each day seems leafy now,
ardent, ordered.
Even sweeping with the old kitchen broom,
the feel of it in my hands,
like pleasure. And the classrooms
which arrived like a daily blow, lined
with the unforgiving faces of the young,
hum now with delicate silence;
a voice, a flicker of understanding
weaving imperishable wheat.
Of course this may all be foolishness
but it's more than a mood, I'm sure,
and I'm going to hang onto it if I can.
That bead, that fruit, that excrescence,
that olive I didn't know I was tending,
breaking from the grey tree,
bathing everything in retrospective oil.

A SAVOR

Darkness casts out darkness, so
they say. But if it's worth anything,
darkness should also beget a little light.
Meanwhile, we're tired of all the harrowing emotions
begetting themselves in the mirror,
ricocheting endlessly. As if
there were no wall behind the mirror,
no good bricks and clay,
rafters and laths
doing their job without complaining,
holding up the house.

It's true we've all suffered quite a lot,
crossed by our own dark intentions,
the intense cruelty of the world
which doesn't seem to know what it's doing
but it has always been so, hasn't it?
And that's what we're here for, isn't it,
to suffer? To realize, in the same instant,
how indecently happy we are.

So I think, in a clarity, a sudden quiet.
Rain suddenly at the window,
saturating the old shingles,
a gurgling, a freshening, a loosening
going on. Whereupon I suddenly remember
a room in a Turgenev novel—
hemp seed and mint and fennel
blowing from an old wooden bureau,
a siskin rattling its yellow cage
hung from a peg in the ceiling.
And underneath, two or three people standing

who have known each other for a long time.
Their faces aren't clear. I don't remember their names,
or even the name of Turgenev's novel.
I see them, nevertheless, standing
under the siskin's cage, smiling,
barely touching, not saying anything.

They don't need to say anything really,
they have known each other
for such a long time. And if they're troubled,
which they are—their hearts
aching with certain inviolable griefs,
the difficulty of living, of being human,
it's not something to talk about.
A savor rises from their clothes, their hands.

Photograph by Ron Trinca

About the Author

Barbara Moore is a graduate of Bennington College and the Syracuse University Writing Program. She has studied with W. H. Auden, Theodore Roethke, and Stanley Kunitz. Her first collection of poems, *The Passionate City*, was published by Hoffstadt Press in 1979. Currently, she teaches literature and creative writing at Le Moyne College, Syracuse, New York.

About the Artist

A native Washingtonian, Carole Clem studied at the Corcoran School of Art. Her photographs have been exhibited in galleries such as the Vision Gallery in San Francisco, the Arc Gallery in Chicago, and the Foundry Gallery in Washington, DC.

Other Books in the Word Works Series:

Alenier, Karren L.	*Wandering on the Outside*
Beall, J. H.	*Hickey, the Days . . .*
*Bradley, John	*Love-In-Idleness: The Poetry of Roberto Zingarello*
*Bursk, Christopher	*The Way Water Rubs Stone*
Cavalieri, Grace	*Creature Comforts*
Cavalieri, Grace	*Swan Research*
Cochrane, Shirley	*Family and Other Strangers*
Fisher, Harrison	*Curtains for You*
*Goldberg, Barbara	*Berta Broadfoot and Pepin the Short: A Merovingian Romance*
**McEuen, James	*Snake Country*
Sargent, Robert	*Aspects of a Southern Story*
Sargent, Robert	*A Woman from Memphis*
*Shomer, Enid	*Stalking the Florida Panther*
**Tham, Hilary	*Bad Names for Women*

*Washington Prize Winners
**Capital Collection

Word Works Anthologies:

Alenier, Karren L.	*Whose Woods These Are*
Bursk, Christopher	*Cool Fire* (A chapbook from the Center for Creative Non-Violence workshop)
Dor, Moshe	
Goldberg, Barbara	
Leshem, Giora	*The Stones Remember* (forthcoming)
Parry, Betty	*The Unicorn and the Garden*

Requests for our brochure and other information must be accompanied by a self-addressed stamped envelope.